Bull at a Gate

Jess Thoroughgood

BookLeaf Publishing

Presentation by *BookLeaf Publishing*

Web: www.bookleafpub.com

E-mail: info@bookleafpub.com

ISBN: 9789357616980

First edition 2022

For The Dream Team. You are my world.

ACKNOWLEDGEMENT

I am writing this book in acknowledgement of all women living on the Autistic Spectrum. To the little girls who are a "pleasure to teach" and the women who are "so organised" and "go above and beyond" in everything they do. I know the pressure you put on yourselves, I know that if you are seen as less than perfect, you feel so much less than worthy. I sit with you in the darkness, when sensory stimulation is overwhelming, and your cup is overflowing. To the women who rehearse every word they publicly say, practice their body language and expressions in a desperate attempt to fit in amongst their peers. The women who struggle to be touched but will hug others to provide them with comfort. To those seen as "gifted" or "a natural" yet are constantly battling to see their own worth. Officially diagnosed or not, you know you are different, you know who you are, and you know yourself better than any of those who have disregarded your struggles. I see you! I know this doesn't describe even a fraction of what it is to live on the spectrum and everyone's experience is unique. If even one person can relate to my writing, then that's a huge win for Aspie Queens ♥

PREFACE

My daughter hates when I tell her that she is like a bull at a gate because it often comes after a completely unnecessary yet heroic feat which has left her bruised and at times bloody, however this term isn't always a negative. She is also often the first to love, the first to help and the first to express herself. So, throughout this book, I am hoping to borrow just a fraction of her courage and tackle this challenge like a BULL AT A GATE.

Yesterday

I let you hurt me,
Yesterday when you mattered,
Today I'm healing.

Sleep

Closing my tired eyes,
And resting my weary feet,
The house is still and peaceful,
Yet I cannot get to sleep.

Instead, I lay in silent frustration,
As I critically examine my faults,
Past mistakes floating through my mind,
Like a heart-wrenching tortuous waltz.

With the hopes of self-forgiveness,
Forever out of reach,
I curl up on my side,
And peaceful sleep beseech.

Smile

Smile, agree, be there for them,
Support them until the end,
Dependability defines your worth,
You are such a wonderful friend.

Your blood is worth bottling,
We're so lucky you are here,
Don't let them see you struggling,
Your smile must always be clear.

They need your kind words and understanding,
Never your troubles or fears,
"Of course, it's no problem", you assure them again,
As you privately wipe your tears.

Always helping yet left unsupported,
By those who hold you so dear,
When your world is in shadow and it hurts to breathe,
You'll be the only one here.

Bliss

It's safe to say,
The more you shout,
The more tension in your day.

If your demeanor is nothing but tough,
I must protest without a doubt,
It won't be long before they've had enough.

Before you blow your proverbial top,
You should listen to this,
Shouts and demands will get things done,
But it's sweeter to live in bliss.

Stars

You were the endless current of tears,
You were the dream that didn't come true,
The hushed voices sharing your story,
The sympathetic stares of those who knew.

You were the stillness as we held you,
And caressed your delicate hands,
Your funeral and tiny coffin,
The mourners watching our grief expand.

You were the sleeping pills each night,
As your Daddy begged me to rest,
You were the concerned frown from Grandma,
As I grew dangerously depressed.

You were my desperate plea to follow you,
My determination to shoulder the blame,
It was my job to protect you always,
Regardless of what the doctor may claim.

You are my joy in your brothers and sister,
The strength and support from your dad,
This new life I'm waking up to,
Starts to resemble the one that I had.

You are the connection amongst your siblings,
As they forgive unintended faux pas,
You are the implied "I love you",
As you dance amongst the stars.

Love

I'm stumbling backwards,
Trusting you'll always catch me,
Forever cocooned.

Learn

Courage to stand and be counted,
Courage to know your worth,
Talent shines brightly from within you,
So claim your place on this earth.

You question praise from others,
You need to learn your truth,
Start seeing strength in assumed weakness,
The future sparks from our youth.

Learn to see your struggles,
As the lessons that they are,
Learning is living,
They don't need to scar.

Breath, relax, but keep moving forward,
Allow yourself time,
The world is patiently waiting for you,
And your potential sublime.

Aspie

You'll like me until you get to know me,
That's when you'll see,
The quirks I try so hard to hide,
That's the real me.

I share too much, stress too much,
Constant eye contact freaks me out,
It feels like my brain is burning,
When you slam things and shout.

I smile so that you'll feel comfortable,
I'll almost always agree,
Masking is how I hide,
You'll only get the best from me.

Unless we are close, please don't touch me,
Because it seriously makes me itch,
And for the love of God say what you mean,
I can't tell if you're a sarcastic bitch.

Inevitably like an old microwave,
My efforts start to snap and spark,
My metaphorical cup overflowing,
I go home to sit alone in the dark.

Raised in a neuro typical household,
Being punished for stimming and inquest,
Always confused as to what I'd done wrong,
Constant failure leads to little rest.

I now live in the house of Autism,
where we support, listen and understand,
At home we embrace the wonder of weirdness,
And live life hand in hand.

Choice

The house you were born in wasn't filled with
love,
Instead anguish and spite,
Don't let them harden your heart,
Keep heading towards the light.

Their pain is not your fault,
It was with them before you were born,
You've given all the love you have,
Your life is ready to dawn.

You weren't born to live in their darkness,
This was never your choice,
They have found a home amongst the shadows,
While you've kept only love in your voice.

You welcomed them into your circle,
Their anger wouldn't let them stay,
They tried to pull you with them,
But you must continue on your way.

Leave them to their sorrows,
You've served time yet it wasn't your trial,
Baby straighten your crown,
It's time for your joy revival.

Alone

I wish you luck,
As I drift away,
With many words unspoken,
Yet nothing left to say.

You were important to me,
For quite a while,
Your name on my phone,
Usually met with a smile.

We enjoyed each lunch date,
And group get together,
Take care now,
And I'll see you never.

Conversations became one sided,
Sliding my phone to ignore,
Planning again to see you,
Held the weight of a chore.

Like a common melody,
That's the way the record plays,
We connect for a moment,
Then go our separate ways.

After mutual texts to cancel,
True plans are shown,
At the end of the day,
I'd rather stay at home.

You say you understand,
You think it's me you see,
With my walls safely unbroken,
I was more of you than me.

Treat

I found a mars bar wrapper on a sanitary box,
And it really made me wonder,
Who chooses to get their chocolate fix,
In this box named for thunder.

Were you rushed off your feet?
Did you not want to share your treat?
Were you in a moment of diet defeat?
Did you find it on the seat?

Has life gotten so incredibly busy,
That your daily routine makes you dizzy?
Had you saved it in your purse,
For when your day couldn't get any worse.

Did you inhale it in just one bite?
Or savour every swallow?
Did you enjoy your moment of retreat
Until the packet was completely hollow?

I guess the town library's toilet,
Is the best seat in the joint
With privacy and door to door service,
And its minimalistic decor on point.

Did you spare a thought,
To your neighbouring porcelain patrons?
Blissfully unaware,
Of your curious feasting innovations.

Whatever your motivation,
I hope it sweetened your day,
Next time put the wrapper in the bin,
Before you head off on your way.

Showtime

I've read and reread my script,
Memorising every page,
My moment is fast approaching,
Almost time to take the stage.

My costume pressed and ready,
My props are all at hand,
Infront of faceless strangers,
That's my place to stand.

The curtain begins to open,
As my excitement starts to build,
The audience waits in silence,
Though every seat is filled.

I discretely tap my microphone,
Ensuring my voice will be heard,
So many months of practice,
To remember every word.

My fellow performers flow about the stage,
Enacting the motions rehearsed,
Taking our voyeurs on a gripping journey,
Of which we are all well versed.

With blinding lights transporting us,
To worlds far and wide,
And the echoing mantra "The show must go on",
Leaving nowhere left to hide.

We reach the conclusion of our story,
Enjoy our moments to bow,
Delight in the words of congratulations,
Our audience is gracious enough to endow.

Towels

Why are bath towels so boring?
When we use them every day,
Which Boorish Beatrice decided this?
To the hum drum I say "Nay".

Beach towels are brilliantly bright,
A sensational colour delight,
Yet tragically they sit in the cupboard,
As we use drab and dreary each night.

Who is responsible for this blunder?
I demand to be told,
I've check shops and online stores,
Everywhere these tedious towels are sold.

I demand it be publicly noted,
That the wearisome has been promoted,
A ghastly decree has been quoted,
With the fabulously flamboyant demoted.

I lay awake at night pondering,
What does that say about us as a society?
How much longer must we survive in this state,
Of sullen style starved sobriety?

Now it's time to stand as one,
For the sake of our children things must change,
Together we must march to our bathrooms,
Our linen cupboards are long overdue a
rearrange.

Throw out your stale and stodgy,
Donate your arid and asinine,
No longer kept for the seldom seaside soiree,
Beach towels it's your time to shine.

Redirected

You follow the rules so carefully,
As chaos is stalking you,
You paint your world with lavender,
But it turns a cyclonic hue.

A butterfly flapped its wings,
Technology zapped and glitched,
An unchecked box in an ivory tower,
And suddenly your plans are switched.

Some believe they have control,
That they hold tight to the reins,
But the universe has other ideas,
And it will always break through those chains.

All you can do is weather the storm,
As you are lashed by a sensory tornado,
Lights brighter and sounds amplifying,
As your brain turns to moldy mashed potato.

Brain pounding,
Alarms sounding,
Brightness surrounding,
Everyone relying,
Anxiety denying,

There will be no crying,
You must keep trying.

Masking level a million,
Difficulty set to extreme,
Present your calm, practiced illusion,
As you internalise every scream.

Shadows

You can't rewind the tape,
You can't press reset,
The shadows from your childhood,
Will never let you forget.

Critical words repeated,
Doesn't make them true,
Yet you let those lies rest,
In the depths of you.

You've let them win long enough,
This will not be your dreams goodnight,
For that blossoming soul you once were,
You have to reignite the fight.

Not with an army of the broken,
Not with fury and rage,
But with the wisdom of knowing who you are,
That shines brightly with the scars of age.

So, sing your karaoke,
Go and write your book,
With your eyes wide open,
Take another look.

It's time to close the curtains,
On the home movies in your mind,
Start living for the future,
For what the film reel could not confine.

Dreams

You hit the ground running,
On the lookout for your next ride,
With endless dreams waiting,
As you struggle to decide.

Without a parachute or helmet,
You're unbuckled and ready to leap,
Without a snorkel or oxygen tank,
You're eager to dive the deep.

So ready for the future,
To discover what lies ahead,
You're missing the rainbows of today,
Please pause and smell the roses instead.

Your career will wait patiently,
As the wind rustles through your hair,
The worlds you are destined to master,
Will profit from life's wear and tear.

The future will laugh and cry with you,
Listen in awe of the stories you'll tell,
Your dreams will embrace you wholly,
Knowing you've lived so well.

So, take your time,
Explore the joys of breathing,
Inevitability is looming,
And with time you will be leaving.

Binge

A bottomless pit of shows,
To scroll and binge all day,
Just sit back, relax, get comfortable,
And watch the pictures play.

Episode after episode,
Season after season,
Put your feet up and take it easy,
You don't even need a reason.

Alphabetised, genre categorised,
You can search by actors too,
Oh, glorious apps on my smart TV,
Is there nothing you can't do.

Netflix doesn't care if you've brushed your hair,
Stan digs your daggy pajamas,
Fluffy socks and dressing gowns,
Are perfect for comedies, Sci-Fis and dramas.

Lock the front door and silence your phone,
Tedious interruptions are undesired,
Right now, I'm in the mood for Avengers and musicals,
Ok Disney plus your hired.

Sorry

The music too loud,
The lights brightly seared,
I thought I had it handled,
Until my control ultimately disappeared.

Attempting to push through,
Until my anxiety alarm started wailing,
Pounding on my brain,
Like relentless icicles hailing.

Taking deep breaths,
While trying to relax my shoulders,
Was much easier,
When the sparks of disquiet were at a smolder.

Trapped by my insecurities,
That people are going to see,
My struggle to appear normal,
While my quirks fight to burst free.

I was ready to escape,
When you innocently asked your question,
Instead of detonating in private,
I exploded in your direction.

For my moment of indiscretion,
I will live with deep regret,
Hoping that my sincere apology,
Will help you to forget.

Unfortunately, this isn't the first time,
And undoubtedly won't be the last,
That my sensory sensitivities,
Will expose me as the outcast.

Safe

You rub my back and scratch my head,
To help me fall asleep,
While my thoughts are off and racing,
Your comfort lulls me to the deep.

On nights when anxiety is winning,
You sooth my mind with your recital,
Of Jack and his magic beans,
This has become our calming cycle.

To the world you are calm and collected,
Quick to laugh amongst the norm,
For me you are strength and security,
As we fight together through every storm.

I can't imagine a day without you,
I hear whispers of home in your voice,
To build our world as one,
Will always be my choice.

Your warmth emanates from inside you,
When enveloped in your embrace,
You love me with such devotion,
Thank you for being my safe place.

Trying

I know you are trying,
Desperate to do what's right,
I can see you need to rest,
I'll carry your confusion through the night.

In the morning we'll try again,
To talk through the miscommunication,
Our desire to understand,
Holding back yesterday's frustration.

Forever my little boy,
Covered in mud and dirt,
Before my eyes becoming a young man,
Through your bravado I see the hurt.

Hurt by disappointment,
Hurt by being misheard,
Hurt by unachievable expectations,
When misunderstandings have occurred.

Please wait a little longer,
Learn your lessons along the way,
When your struggles transform into
understanding,
That will be your day.

The light in you is brilliant,
Your laughter is a rainbow unfurled,
With your smile shining brightly,
You light up the whole world.

Soul

You take on each day,
With wisdom and understanding,
As an old soul remembering,
And past lives trials withstanding.

With humour and comedic timing,
Of a gentleman way beyond your years,
Your sass and innovation,
Leaving us with laughter's tears.

You never miss an opportunity,
To remind us of your love,
As you groove against the current,
And give your boundaries another shove.

Everyone that meets you,
Is bewitched by your empathy and grace,
With your perception and insight overflowing,
Your spirit impossible to replace.

I love you as my baby,
I admire your world view,
I can't wait to see where life takes you,
Little Man this one's for you.

www.ingramcontent.com/pod-product-compliance
Lightning Source LLC
Chambersburg PA
CBHW062203160726
48282CB00027B/983
* 9 7 8 9 3 5 7 6 1 6 9 8 0 *